Cycles

Dan McPeake

BookLeaf Publishing

India | USA | UK

Presentation by *BookLeaf Publishing*

Web: www.bookleafpub.com

E-mail: info@bookleafpub.com

ISBN: 978-93-5744-890-1

First edition 2022

ACKNOWLEDGEMENT

Thank you to Bookleaf Publishing for allowing me to make this happen. Much appreciation to all of my fellow writers and readers who have supported my creative journey.

PREFACE

These poems were all written at different points in my life. Some are a few months old, others over a decade. I chose them because connected, they tell a story. Some are visceral, others more imagistic. Combined, they are cycles.

Lift Off

Cracks
In the surface of time
Meander into the sunrise
The bosom of the earth
Breathes,
Sighs
Listlessly waits
For the upcoming travellers
Red giants peek through
Heating of the hands
of the lost and innocent
Milliseconds slow
cease and fade
Stillness penetrates
An exhale
Gaia begins anew

Collision Course

One vessel collides
with another
as the tissue enters an altered state
continuously pumping
Panting
pumping
panting
It vacillates in circles
Molecular weight is shifting
As one becomes two
Pulsating
vibrations echoing in the moonlight
Globules of sweat
filling the room with condensation
Exhales of joy,
frenetic excitement
it all blurs together

Speck

Faded dust
Speckled in the wind
Teaming with heaps
Of somersaults and spiders
Pressing backward with a yellow hue
Rowboats in the mist
Dying
Milking the water
Creating a ripple effect
A crescent-shaped hologram
Of diamonds in the rough
Flaming shoulders sparkle
Then extinguished
To create a landscape
Frozen in time

Band Practice

I can hear the trumpets
Tubas
and trombones
dignifying the air
with their pumps and scratches
of virginal fortitude.
The horns and the flutes
sputtering
in galaxial corners
wafting
with immature brevity.
Reeds,
sanctioned by
an off-key clarinet
clashing against the timpani
release a symphonic
cacophony
One
Two
Three
Four
a mashup of skill sets
breathes new life
filling the pockets,
airholes

of woodwinds and brass
churning
punting
panting
creating.

Foggy Dew

Curtains
Flummoxed by their weight
holding back the light
Breathes upon
the panes of glass
Fogging
The Painful view
of velveteen drapes
pulled back
crawling towards
the edges of a moonbeam
disguised as happiness
a sensorial reflection
overcome by peace

Black Rain

Gunpowder filled the sky
While the boats fill up the seas
A fortified lake of solitude
Ash coming down in buckets

A shoreline created by cannonballs
Riflery and ropes
The smoke curls towards the sun
A blinding hue of darkness

The melodic cacophony of battle
Heave-ho heave-ho the warrior cries
Drowning
Reaching the abyss

Light has poked through
The clouds of sorrows
Until finally
Freedom??

Aimless

An upturned smile glistens,
Reflects
In the conscious mind of an aimless wanderer
A shimmering, shivering
emotive presence
Eternal beauty is a flame
Running,
racing
betwixt and between
two fluttering hearts
washing away the sadness
living for today

Waltz of the Proletariat

Mic check!
(drop)
Mic check!
(drop)
We are the army of civilizations
Fighting against the cacophonous
commercialization
Wandering in a zombie state
Restless stillness
of droopy-eyed robots

An industrial complex of hate
An uprising of love
Tent city flashmob
Dance until death
RepeatThe myth of loyalty
Remains in the ethereal ether of time
Hurtling outwards from the cortex
From cerebral to the conscious
Passive to reactive
And then…
BOOM go the footsteps

Cycles

downvotes and doomscrolls
likes and re-tweets
instafilters and pins
and vegan fake meat

lip-dubs on tik-tok
the cycle of news
re-runs and repeats
filmed with skeleton crews

clash of the titans
streamers galore
pining for freedom
wanting more more more

No more theatres to sit in
No more tables to wait
a multitude of rules
leads to a disturbing fate

in the darkest hours
of the final dreary days
brings a new cistern
to get over this craze

Reaching new lows
and touching impossibly high
it's time to say hello
and acknowledge goodbye

so upvotes and pleasures
of a life built on memes
maybe the world will wake
And it will have been a dream

Fake News

Playing soccer in the streets
While behind
smashed windows,
flaming cars
lumped together with the crowds
By the uneducated
uninitiated
uninformed

The madness of the mob
Overwhelms the anonymity
of uninspired intoxication
A breeding ground of confusion
leads to a conflation of intrusion
For we are the true rebels
Who look the other way
A peaceful plasticine moment

Story time
Blaring screens in every home
Catastrophically spreading (mis) information
Ignorantly (mis) leading the people
Chaotic
Anarchic
Criminal

and all bullshit

Whisked away by the souls of the insignificant
Fighting for the name
For the (true) identity
Giving the middle finger to society
Suspected destroyers
Secretly nice
Dismantling the damage
Of patriarchal norms

The Killing of Abraham

Existence is futile
Rumspringa, rumspringa
As life pulls you away
From the bearded wonders of the world

The father
waiting, commanding, decreeing
Thou shall not
yada yada yada

The son
fulfilling his destiny
suffering
no "daughter" in sight

The holy Ghost
is the one who waits
should he be so kind
an awkward figure indeed

The offshoots
claiming to know better

Re-writing history
upon new discoveries

the modifiers
the thinkers
the proselytizers
A reclamation proclamation

The originals
who wrote the book of laws
erased and persecuted
a detailed description

One rules over all
the other, overruled
except in the holy land
behind the walls of merged worlds

400 years
the prophet came along
a new enemy has arisen
diverging visions

1, 2, 3,
yet plenty more to come
1, 2, 3,
it's uphill from here

some 37 000 adaptations

without a consensus view
both accepting and restricting
a literal interpretive dance
steal, kill, lie, cheat
covet, witness, honour, infallibility
Baruch atah adonai
Allah akhbar

So many branches
leads to a dying tree
it cannot hold its weight
it is stretched way too thin

There were the protestors
the baptizers
the rebels
each trying for a stronghold

Fighting for humanity's moral compass
the way in which to live
entangling beliefs
all juxtaposed together

The truth is unknown
lying somewhere in between
A little of this, a little of that
For a little goes a long way

1, 2, 3, 4

books to tell the tale
1, 2, 3, 4
billion stars to ponder

this battle is not yet over
has it even begun
the convergence of ideas
past, present, and future

Time
the answer lies in time
a far-off place
yet steps away

The discovery
will simultaneously strengthen and weaken
but really it will not react
for the something is entirely nothing at all

existence is futile
Rumspringa, rumspringa
As life pulls you away
From the bearded wonders of the world

Trigger

Unconscious memories
Not lies but neither truths
half-worn formed
over time, years
situations
both stark and vague
simultaneously culprit and victim
interrupting the senses
invading the grey matter
entrenched within societal norms
formed
by an outdated plan of action
complete with a violent realization
simple microaggressions
spirally converge
inside a tortured mind
trying to make peace
with what's behind
 but it's also
time to find
the inner truth
Anxiety
a continued digging of malevolence
trying to hide
suppress

but also
to confess
a jumping of emotions
thoughts
intruding on happiness
only to cause chaos
rightfully
in how we remember
the actions of others
versus
ourselves
deciding
who, what, when, where, how
a confession of entitlementbegins the wet
madness
which is
condescendingly dismissive
a bold catch from long ago
a yesteryear of sorts
time flies when no one pays attention
or mentions
a past
of small discernible acts
Haunted
by the facts
evidence of impropriety
we become fiery
a designation of resignation
we are stationed

to forget
and yet
the mind is a powerful step
the ladders of power
are burning
like grenfell tower
the bourgeoisie elite are busy
with their powders
galavanting
delicate flowers
a symptom
within a system
cause and effect
it's time to pay our debts
a reset
cleaning up the faults
of multiple assaults
halt
exhale
just breathe
a little deeper
our time has come
the reckoning is beckoning
with implosions of emotions
infections of reflections
each other
all sisters and brothers
go figure
Rise Up

Pull the trigger!

Fallen

Crumbs,
slipping through a festooned collarbone
warbling echoes
of an aborted revolution.
Simmering lightsmuted,
masking
the crater of liberty
fallen
upturned and dishevelled
Polluted streets
desecrated graves
the soldiers of fortune
whisked to another plain
reborn as warriors of peace
Fallen
Rebooted
designed
covered with ashes, ammo
buried beneath the snow
Discarded rucksacks
torn, shredded
no longer a symbol
of deluded and devoted honesty
traipsed along discoloured stones
weighted with grief, sorrow

eroding
implanted memories
of manufactured freedom

Flame

Port-wine sunset
Strips beneath the scattered leaves
The air is crisp
Dying with frozen agitation
Rendered speechless
By the winds of the moon
Clouds of the beached sand
Upon which
The gull relapses
Bequeathing his legacy
To the otters and seals
Of the wind-chilled shores
The sky's smokey hue
Blasphemed
Trolling towards ecstasy

Seasons

The daffodil wilts
As the sun fails
The juniper blooms
In the smouldering moonlight
The light of fireflies,
Evaporate the mothballs
And for a while,
Silence

Nothing Left

The life that is
Is not the life that should be
The powers that are
Be the powers are not
The words that aren't
Make the words you can
The world you want
Not the world we are

The truth that is
Just spoken lies
The time we give
The time we get
This is the time
There is nothing left

If nothing was had
Nothing would be wanted
You have the powers that be
Not no king nor deity
The world be lost
The people gone
No heroes, no mortals
The forgotten saved

The rules of the wise
The ways of the dumb
The strong, the weak
The rich, the poor
Walking together
Through the door

Both Sides Now: A Mathematical Proposition

Society is not a parallelogram
When it comes to sharing blame
A tornado of incoherent stupidity
Sand-blown fields of destruction

Civility has become a trapezoid
A rhombus in an ellipsoidal void
An isosceles of equality
Exposed to the elements

The population is a polygon
Each sharing topological space
Building towards a fifth dimension
Manifesting interconnectivity

Simultaneously hyper speed
Yet a wink and a crawl
Feeling like a Klein bottle
Angrily incomplete

The globe is now a Torus
Falling into a gaping black hole
With no end in sight
Bringing about a supernova

Sky Blue

A mystic sunrise
Flurries of red and gold
Explosive
Making way
For ol blue yonder
Sky blue
Spreading across the seas
Sky blue
Wandering through the trees
Sprinting, shooting, running, racing
All through the day
Until it sleeps
Returning again
To a mystic sunrise

Beneath The Shadows Of The Sun

The light is fading
My head is spinning
For once there is silence
of many moons past
Withering through hellish nights
Fraying speckles of humanity
To keep in time with others

It is demonstrative
To be alone
Revelling in misfortune
A quaint suffering
a quiet tear
For it is not to be a graceful exit
Or, a grand entrance

The only wait
Is crossing the threshold
over a moonlit valley
Beneath the shadows of the sun

We wallow, we follow
The desert tribe
The sand grasping our toes
Lingering on,
Each grain of life form
awaiting the senses
Of a camelback Bedouin

For once the stars shine
Far across the plain
Reaching to the seas
Sailing over the honking navy
Descending in a freefall
Crashing,
Landing
Beneath the shadows of the sun

The morning after
The fallen is forgotten
A diminutive sleight-of-hand
to wash away the guilt

What has become of us?
The land of golden opportunity
Blackened by the sorrows of old
and ignorance of the new

A final saying

of effortless destruction
Peek-a-boo
Peek-a-boo
It's good to see you too
If only for a nanosecond
of time,
space,
Beneath the shadows of the sun

End of the Road

A distant far-away future
Of memories not yet determined
Breathes new life
A circular, peculiar
multi-universal dimension
Standing
On the tip of a rocky exclave
Dewdrops, ash
Life
Birthing the landscape below
What was old is new again
Born
Free
In an infinite loop

Creation

Sisyphus freebased on Mount Olympus
While Zeus watched from on high
Atlas shrugged and shook his head
Archimedes ran naked nearby

Aristotle philosophised
Hercules tried to be strong
Ptolemy erred and erred
Helen(a) of Troy joined the throngs

Oedipus loved his mother
And Icarus burnt his wings
And Joseph Campbell wrote it all down
And now they all are kings

Pegasus flew and took to the skies
While Gaia guarded the seas
Hades stood at the gates of Hell
Is this how we came to be?

www.ingramcontent.com/pod-product-compliance
Lightning Source LLC
LaVergne TN
LVHW010926200726
843509LV00013B/2102